SALADS

HAMLYN

COOK'S NOTES

OVEN TEMPERATURES

°C	°F	GAS MARK	
70 C	150 F	Low	–
80 C	175 F	Low	–
90 C	190 F	Low	–
100 C	200 F	¼	–
110 C	225 F	¼	Very slow
130 C	250 F	½	Very slow
150 C	275 F	1	Slow
160 C	300 F	2	Moderately slow
170 C	325 F	3	Moderately slow
180 C	350 F	4	Moderate
190 C	375 F	5	Moderately hot
200 C	400 F	6	Hot
220 C	425 F	7	Hot
230 C	450 F	8	Very hot
240 C	475 F	9	Very hot

MICROWAVE POWER SETTINGS

Power Level	Percentage	Numerical Setting
HIGH	100%	9
MEDIUM HIGH	75%	7
MEDIUM	50%	5
DEFROST	30%	3
LOW	10%	1

SOLID WEIGHT CONVERSIONS

METRIC	IMPERIAL
15 g	½ oz
25 g	1 oz
50 g	2 oz
100 g	4 oz/¼ lb
175 g	6 oz
225 g	8 oz/½ lb
350 g	12 oz
450 g	1 lb
575 g	1¼ lb
700 g	1½ lb
800 g	1¾ lb
900 g	2 lb

MICROWAVE

Microwave tips have been tested using a 650 watt microwave oven. Add 15 seconds per minute for 600 watt ovens and reduce the timings by 5-10 seconds per minute for 700 watt ovens.

LIQUID VOLUME CONVERSIONS

METRIC	IMPERIAL
25 ml	1 fl oz
50 ml	2 fl oz
125 ml	4 fl oz
150 ml	5 fl oz/¼ pt
175 ml	6 fl oz
225 ml	8 fl oz
300 ml	10 fl oz/½ pt
450 ml	15 fl oz/¾ pt
600 ml	20 fl oz/1pt
900 ml	1½ pt
1.2 l	2 pt
1.7 l	3 pt

AUSTRALIAN CUP CONVERSIONS

	METRIC	IMP
1 cup flour	150 g	5 oz
1 cup sugar, granulated	225 g	8 oz
1 cup sugar, caster	225 g	8 oz
1 cup sugar, icing	175 g	6 oz
1 cup sugar, soft brown	175 g	6 oz
1 cup butter	225 g	8 oz
1 cup honey, treacle	350 g	12 oz
1 cup fresh breadcrumbs	50 g	2 oz
1 cup uncooked rice	200 g	7 oz
1 cup dried fruit	175 g	6 oz
1 cup chopped nuts	100 g	4 oz
1 cup desiccated coconut	75 g	3 oz
1 cup liquid	250 ml	9 floz

WEIGHTS AND MEASURES

Metric and Imperial weights and measures are given throughout. Don't switch from one to the other within a recipe as they are not interchangeable. 1 tsp is the equivalent of a 5 ml spoon and 1 tbls equals a 15 ml spoon.

All spoon measurements are level, all flour plain, all sugar granulated and all eggs medium unless otherwise stated.

SYMBOLS

 FREEZER TIP

 SERVING SUGGESTION

 MICRO-WAVE TIP

 WINE & DRINK NOTE

CONTENTS

Front Jacket Photography: James Murphy

First published in Great Britain 1993
by Hamlyn
an imprint of Reed Consumer Books Limited
Michelin House, 81 Fulham Road, London SW3 6RB
and Auckland, Melbourne, Singapore and Toronto

ISBN 0 600 57774 0

A CIP catalogue for this book is available at the British Library

Produced by Mandarin Offset
Printed and Bound in Singapore

SALADS & DRESSINGS

The wonderful array of interesting salad leaves now available has given that old favourite 'the green salad' a huge fillip. Use them in any combination that suits your whim. Almost any leaf, from crisp Chinese leaves to tender lamb's lettuce will do excellently. But any dressing certainly won't.

Get the dressing right

Vinaigrettes (or French dressings) don't have to be rigidly classical. Use tasteless vegetable oil (like peanut oil or corn oil) for most salads, but vary the flavourings to suit the ingredients and your mood. You could add mustard to the dressing for potatoes, chopped coriander for fish, garlic and mint for beans, and so on.

Crisp and dry

Remember not to overdo the dressing. Make enough to coat each leaf, but not enough to collect in the bottom of the salad bowl. This is one cause of the commonest problem with salads - soggy leaves. If every leaf is not thoroughly dried, the dressing becomes watery and insipid and the leaves go glassy and limp in the bottom of the bowl. A salad spinner is one answer: no more bruising the delicate leaves as you dab away with a tea-towel.

Salad leaves

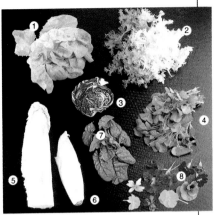

1 Iceberg (Webb's wonder)
Crisp lettuce that keeps well, with a high proportion of tender, pale inner leaves. Not much taste but excellent texture.

2 Rocket
Dark, pretty leaf with strong peppery taste. Best used to spike bland salads.

3 Oak-leaf
Tender, expensive, and doesn't keep long, but delicious and very pretty. To wash, hold by stalk and submerge gently in cold water. Leave to drain upside-down.

4 Cos
Sweet, crisp, long large leaves. Keeps excellently. The inner leaves have the best flavour.

5 Lamb's lettuce (corn salad)
Tender mini-plants with a mild flavour. Wash carefully but keep the leaves attached to each other to preserve their pretty shape.

6 Lollo rosso
Similar to oak-leaf but frillier and less tender. Wash gently and spin.

7 Little gem
Related to cos but much smaller. All leaves are crisp and delicious. Split in half, then separate.

1 Hothouse (round)
Tender lettuce and even the darkest leaves are edible. Wash and dry as for oak-leaf.

2 Curly endive
Use the pale inner leaves and discard the dark bitter ones.

3 Radicchio
Pretty, round-headed chicory. Keeps well. Slightly bitter.

4 Watercress
To store watercress, put upside-down (leaves submerged) in cold water in the fridge. Rinse under water while still in the bunch, untied. Use only leafy ends.

5 Chinese leaves
Insipid tasting, but has wonderfully crisp, firm heads. Keeps well.

6 Chicory (Belgian endive)
Split lengthways with a knife and peel off the leaves. Very slightly but pleasantly bitter.

7 Spinach
Young spinach leaves are excellent raw. Old leaves are too tough. Detach the stalk by folding leaf along rib, tearing away stalk.

8 Edible flowers
The young leaves of edible flowers, such as pansies, nasturtium and polyanthus, add a peppery flavour to mixed salads. Leave the tiniest leaves whole but shred the larger ones and use as a herb.

Salad notes

Probably the most important rule in making a good salad is not to be tempted to overdo it. Many a salad is ruined by too many ingredients that are weird and less-than-wonderful. Stick to simple combinations like potato and onion, celery and cheese or tomato and garlic and you can't go wrong.

FIRST COURSE SALAD

Arrange pretty and unusual leaves on individual plates. Top with hot fried croûtons, chicken livers and cubes of fried bacon.

MAIN COURSE SALAD

Shred Chinese leaves, spinach, chicory, and ham slices and cooked chicken into similar thin strips. Toss, dress and sprinkle with walnuts. Serve with bread.

PREPARING SALAD LEAVES

1 Wash tender leaves such as oakleaf or soft hothouse lettuce by holding the whole head of lettuce by the stalk and submerging it in a bowl or sink of cold water. Plunge it gently up and down. Wipe the chicory heads with a damp cloth and break off any discoloured leaves, but don't bother to wash every leaf.

2 Iceberg, radicchio and any cabbage-like crisp lettuce can be pulled apart. Don't cut lettuce or wring it to break up the leaves, as both methods bruise them. Tear the leaves to bits one by one with your fingers. Then wash them. Use a salad spinner to get the leaves really dry.

3 Not more than half an hour before serving, give the dressing jar a shake and toss the salad in the dressing. Use your hands – salad servers bruise tender leaves. Transfer to a bowl, leaving behind excess salad dressing.

Mayonnaise

Mayonnaise, a delicate mixture of egg yolks and oil, has many simple variations and can be used to transform a wide range of meat, fish and salad dishes.

3 Add 1½ tbls vinegar or lemon juice. Then salt and ground white pepper to taste.

WATCHPOINT

RAW EGGS HAVE BEEN FOUND TO CONTAIN THE SALMONELLA FOOD-POISONING ORGANISM. TO REDUCE THE RISKS BUY SALMONELLA-FREE EGGS AND KEEP THE MAYONNAISE COOL AT ALL TIMES. ALSO, MAKE SURE IT HAS A GOOD DASH OF LEMON JUICE OR VINEGAR IN IT.

1 Place 2 egg yolks in a bowl (warm over hot water if cold). Beat with a teaspoon of Dijon mustard.

BLENDER MAYONNAISE

2 Gradually add 175 ml/6 fl oz of salad oil, drip by drip, beating all the time. The mixture will gradually thicken as the oil is added.

TIP

☐ TOO THIN? ADD MORE OIL, BEATING WELL BETWEEN EACH ADDITION.
☐ TOO THICK? ADD 1 TBLS OF WATER JUST BEFORE USING.
☐ IF IT STARTS TO CURDLE, BEAT IN 1-2 TSP BOILING WATER BEFORE ADDING MORE OIL. IF UNSUCCESSFUL, START AGAIN WITH ANOTHER YOLK AND BEAT IN CURDLED MIXTURE VERY GRADUALLY.

Whizz the yolks, seasoning, vinegar or lemon juice in a blender and pour in the oil in a thin steady stream. Use pure olive oil and add plenty of garlic for a Mediterranean dressing. A richer flavoured mayonnaise can be made by substituting half the quantity of salad oil with a nut oil (walnut or hazelnut) and by adding chopped fresh herbs such as tarragon, thyme, chives and chervil. Serve with crudités.

Vinaigrette dressings

Different flavourings, such as garlic, mustard and ginger can be added to this basic oil and wine vinegar dressing to enhance meat, fish, egg and vegetable dishes.

CLASSIC VINAIGRETTE

Put 4 tbls oil, 1 tbls wine vinegar, ½ tsp salt and plenty of freshly ground black pepper in a screw-top jar and shake vigorously.

WALNUT OIL & LIME DRESSING

INGREDIENTS

---

1 FRESH LIME

---

2 TBLS SALAD OIL

---

1 TBLS WALNUT OIL

GOOD PINCH OF ROCK SALT OR SEA SALT

---

10 TWISTS OF THE BLACK PEPPERMILL

---

1 Grate the green part only of the lime skin (not the pith) extremely finely. Squeeze the juice. Combine the grated rind, juice, two oils and seasoning in a screw-top jar and shake.

2 Serve this dressing with any crunchy combination of apples, cabbage or celery, radicchio, chicory or watercress.

HERB & YOGHURT DRESSING

INGREDIENTS

---

4 TBLS SALAD OIL

---

2 TBLS GREEK YOGHURT

---

1 TBLS CHOPPED CHIVES, PARSLEY, TARRAGON, MINT OR CHERVIL, OR A COMBINATION OF ANY OR ALL

GOOD PINCH OF ROCK SALT OR SEA SALT

---

10 TWISTS OF THE BLACK PEPPERMILL

---

1 Whisk the oil into the yoghurt to produce a semi-emulsion. Add the herbs and seasonings.

2 Add to cooked fish strips (such as fresh mackerel fillets), hard-boiled eggs or quails' eggs to make an elegant starter. It also goes well with peeled broad beans (purple skins off) and cooked vegetable salads.

TOMATO & GARLIC DRESSING

INGREDIENTS

4 TBLS VIRGIN OLIVE OIL

1 TBLS TOMATO JUICE (FRESH OR BOTTLED)

1 CLOVE OF GARLIC, CRUSHED

GOOD PINCH OF SEA SALT OR ROCK SALT

½ TSP SUGAR

10 TWISTS OF THE BLACK PEPPERMILL

1 Put ingredients into a screw-top jar and shake. A piquant dressing that is perfect for livening up potato or rice salads, finely shredded red cabbage or cold fish. The strong flavour also complements salads containing sultanas and pine kernels.

TIP

USE FLAVOURED VINEGARS TO PEP UP SALAD DRESSINGS — RED WINE VINEGAR WITH ADDED ROSEMARY OR WHITE WINE VINEGAR WITH TARRAGON. FLAVOURED OILS MAKE GOOD DRESSINGS TOO — OLIVE OIL WITH TOMATO SALADS AND NUT OILS WITH FISH SALADS.

1 Put ingredients into a screw-top jar and shake. Delicious with peeled cherry tomatoes, salad niçoise, cold fish, and cold cooked vegetables, such as potatoes.

SPICY DRESSING

INGREDIENTS

4 TBLS SALAD OIL

1 TBLS LEMON JUICE

1 CLOVE OF GARLIC, CRUSHED

½ TSP GRATED FRESH ROOT GINGER

1 SPRING ONION, FINELY CHOPPED

½ TSP GROUND CARDAMOM

½ TSP GROUND CORIANDER

SPRIG OF FRESH CORIANDER, ROUGHLY CHOPPED

PINCH OF GROUND CUMIN

Flavoured vinegars

Capture the sweet aroma of fresh herbs by preserving their flavour in ordinary vinegars. They are perfect for giving salads an extra lift in the winter.

Good mixers
Vinegars that blend well with herbs and flavourings are red wine, white wine, cider, malt and tarragon wine vinegars.

HERB VINEGARS

Herb vinegars are most appealing if you can flavour them with a variety of home-grown herbs, although many supermarkets now have a wide selection to choose from. Herbs that blend well with white wine vinegar are tarragon, basil, fennel, rosemary, thyme, oregano, marjoram and bay.

RASPBERRY VINEGAR

PREPARATION TIME: 5 MINS
+ MARINATING
MAKES 750 ML/1 ¼ PT VINEGAR

I N G R E D I E N T S

450 G/1 LB FRESH RASPBERRIES

600 ML/1 PT WHITE WINE VINEGAR

1 Reserve 6 raspberries and put the rest in a bowl. Bruise them lightly to release their juices. Pour the vinegar over the berries, cover with a tea-towel and leave at room temperature for 24 hours. Strain the vinegar.

2 Put 6 fresh raspberries into the bottom of a 750 ml/1¼ pt bottle and cover with the strained vinegar. Seal the bottle and allow to stand for 2-3 days before using.

Flavoured oils

There is an increasing variety of oils on the market. Each offer their own distinct flavour to complement your own particular style of cooking.

1. Olive oil – fruity often nutty olive taste. Perhaps the most sought after and well established oil. Ideal for dressings.

2. Walnut oil – rich, with a strong nutty flavour. Best when used in special salad dressings.

3. Groundnut oil – light neutral taste. Suitable for shallow and deep frying and mayonnaise.

4. Safflower oil – delicate taste with a light texture.

HOT CHILLI OIL

Put five chillies in a bottle or jar, cover with 250 ml/9 fl oz of olive or groundnut oil and leave to stand for 2-3 weeks. This oil can be used sparingly to pep up spicy dishes.

HERBAL OILS

To make herbal oils, place your chosen herbs in a bottle or jar, top up with oil and leave to infuse for 3-4 weeks. Try:

1. Olive oil with garlic, rosemary and bay. Use in Mediterranean and barbecue cooking.

2. Groundnut oil or sunflower oil with sage, thyme and winter savory. Ideal for grilled white meats.

3. Safflower oil with fennel stem, dill, garlic and thyme. Use with fish and shellfish.

PEPPERCORN OIL

Heat 3 tbls groundnut or safflower oil in a small frying-pan, add 1 tbls of black peppercorns and sizzle lightly for 3-4 minutes to release their flavour. Transfer to a bottle or jar, add 1 pricked clove of garlic, top up with 175 ml/6 fl oz oil and leave for 2-3 weeks. Try a mixture of black, green and pink peppercorns for a colourful alternative. The oil will impart a wonderful flavour to marinades.

Pretty presentation

Salads should not only taste good, they should look good too. A bowl of unusual leaves, carefully tossed in a delicious dressing, is an attractive and colourful way to start a meal, or to refresh your guests' palates after the main course. But some salads, especially those with heavier ingredients like avocado, tomato, nuts, eggs or fish, look much better carefully arranged on individual plates.

Pasta salad
Combine cooked, drained pasta with seafood such as tuna. Mix together with stoned black olives, finely chopped onion and diced red pepper. Serve with garlicky French dressing and bread.

Herb salad
Leave herb leaves whole if they are young and fresh – tarragon sprigs, thyme leaves or flower sprigs, chervil sprigs, flat-leaved parsley, thin chives – and serve in a mild lettuce salad of iceberg or cos. Dress lightly with French dressing and serve with tomato wedges.

Fruit bowls
Halve a melon and scoop out. Fill with quartered cherry tomatoes and chunks of cucumber. Dress with a mint-flavoured vinaigrette and garnish with mint. Hollowed-out red apples can also be used as containers for chopped crabsticks, celery and a curried mayonnaise. Garnish with coriander.

TIP
ADD DANDELION LEAVES, THE NEW LEAVES OF HAWTHORN, WILD SORREL LEAVES OR EVEN GROUND ELDER LEAVES TO A GREEN SALAD. DO NOT USE DANDELION LEAVES ON THEIR OWN AS THE FLAVOUR IS TOO STRONG.

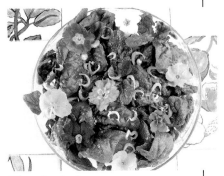

Savoury fruit salad

Use segments of orange and thin slices of melon. Interleave on a plate and flavour with French dressing with green and pink whole peppercorns.

Cheese

Cubed, grated or sliced, cheese can add substance and flavour to a salad. Grated Parmesan goes well with green salads and blue cheese is delicious crumbled into a dressing. Softer, creamier cheeses like ricotta can be added to salad greens and sprinkled with chopped chives and spring onions.

Floral salad

Add borage, nasturtium and clary flowers (or any other edible flowers) to a spinach salad. Sprinkle with sliced chicory.

Potato salads

Potatoes are the ideal ingredient for making a salad more robust. Slice cold boiled new potatoes and mix with cream, lemon juice, slices of celery, strips of ham and mixed fresh herbs (parsley, chives, mint and chervil). New potatoes can also be served with curried or plain mayonnaise.

Goat's cheese salad

Arrange overlapping slices of avocado, slices of firm, ripe tomato and chunks of goat's cheese on a serving plate with chicory or lettuce leaves. Garnish with sprigs of chervil and dress with a light vinaigrette dressing.

WHITE RADISH & CUCUMBER SALAD

Michael Michaels

This shredded side salad is a refreshing contrast to rich and spicy food. Serve tossed in its own delicious dressing.

14

PREPARATION TIME: 10 MINS
SERVES 6

I N G R E D I E N T S

450 G/1 LB CARROTS, PEELED

15 CM/6 IN PIECE CUCUMBER

15 CM/6 IN PIECE MOOLI
(WHITE RADISH)

¼ SMALL WHITE CABBAGE

225 G/8 OZ FIRM, RIPE TOMATOES

FOR THE DRESSING

1 CLOVE OF GARLIC, CRUSHED

4 TBLS LIGHT SOY SAUCE

PINCH CASTER SUGAR

2 TBLS SESAME OIL

GROUND BLACK PEPPER

2 TBLS LEMON JUICE

3 TBLS CHOPPED FRESH CORIANDER,
TO GARNISH

3 Pour dressing over the salad and toss well to coat. Sprinkle over the chopped coriander and serve.

1 Using a sharp knife, shred the carrots, cucumber, mooli and white cabbage very finely. Cut the tomatoes into wedges and toss the vegetables together in a large bowl.

2 Mix the dressing ingredients together in a screw-top jar and shake to combine.

MELONBALL SALAD

Clint Brown

Small balls of goats' cheese, melon and cucumber
offer contrasting textures in this
refreshing salad.

PREPARATION TIME: 20 MINS
SERVES 4

INGREDIENTS

100 G/4 OZ SOFT GOATS' CHEESE
4 TBLS FRESHLY CHOPPED HERBS (BASIL, PARSLEY, CHERVIL)
225 G/8 OZ CHARENTAIS MELON
225 G/8 OZ GALIA MELON
HALF A CUCUMBER, PEELED
HALF A LARGE PAPAYA
100 G/4 OZ BLACK GRAPES
JUICE OF 1 ORANGE
GROUND BLACK PEPPER
8 CHERRY TOMATOES
4 SMALL ROUND RED RADISHES
FRESH SPINACH OR VINE LEAVES, TO SERVE
4 TBLS TASTELESS SALAD OIL

2 Use a small melon baller to scoop the melons, cucumber and papaya into balls. Add the grapes.

3 Sprinkle the melon balls lightly with orange juice and ground black pepper. Hull the cherry tomatoes and remove the root and some of the leaves and stalks from the radishes. Roll the cucumber balls in salad oil.

4 Line a serving dish with spinach or vine leaves and arrange the fruit, vegetables and cheese balls on top. Sprinkle with a little oil and the rest of the orange juice just before serving.

1 Roll the goats' cheese into marble-sized balls and roll in the freshly chopped mixed herbs, so the balls are evenly coated.

TIP

IN ORDER TO MAKE THIS A SWEETER DESSERT SALAD, REPLACE THE RADISHES, CUCUMBER AND TOMATOES WITH BALLS OF APPLE AND PEAR. MIX THE ORANGE JUICE WITH PASSION-FRUIT PULP TO ADD A SWEET TANG.

PALM HEART SALAD

Alan Newnham

Amuse your guests with this visual pun – a picture on a plate. The palm tree is made up of a palm heart – the firm and mild-tasting bud of certain palm trees. Serve with a spicy dressing.

PREPARATION TIME: 15-20 MINS
SERVES 6

I N G R E D I E N T S

400 G/14 OZ TINNED PALM HEARTS

2 RIPE AVOCADOS

2 LARGE RIPE MANGOES

JUICE OF ½ A LIME

½ CUCUMBER, FINELY SHREDDED

FOR THE DRESSING

¼ TSP MILD CURRY POWDER

1 TSP SUGAR

1 TBLS MANGO CHUTNEY, STRAINED

2 TBLS LIME JUICE

6 TBLS OLIVE OIL

SALT AND GROUND BLACK PEPPER

2 Cut six palm hearts into 2.5 cm/1 in pieces and reassemble each one on a serving plate to make up the palm tree trunk. Cut the smaller remaining palm hearts into 6 mm/¼ in slices to make the coconuts.

1 First make the dressing: mix the curry powder, sugar, strained chutney and lime juice together in a bowl. Gradually beat in the olive oil. Season to taste with salt and pepper. Drain the palm hearts.

3 Peel and thinly slice the avocados and mangoes and sprinkle with lime juice. Arrange alternate slices of mango and avocado at the top of each palm tree trunk to form the leaves. Then lay the thin slices of palm heart at the centre of the leaves to make the coconuts. Arrange the shredded cucumber along the bottom of the tree to complete the picture and serve with the dressing.

TIP

PALM HEARTS ARE AVAILABLE IN TINS FROM DELICATESSENS. IF YOU ARE UN-ABLE TO BUY THEM USE COOKED LEEKS.

STRAWBERRY & CUCUMBER SALAD

Michael Michaels

Strawberries in a savoury salad? This may sound odd but it is actually superbly refreshing as a side dish.

PREPARATION TIME: 10 MINS
SERVES 4

INGREDIENTS

FOR THE SALAD

100 G/4 OZ FRESH DATES

225 G/8 OZ STRAWBERRIES, HULLED
AND SLICED

½ CUCUMBER, THINLY SLICED

FRESH MINT SPRIGS, TO GARNISH

FOR THE DRESSING

125 ML/4 FL OZ LOW-FAT YOGHURT

1 TBLS FRESHLY CHOPPED MINT

1 TBLS STRAWBERRY SYRUP

SALT AND GROUND BLACK PEPPER

3 Mix together all the dressing ingredients in a bowl. Drizzle over the salad and garnish with the fresh mint sprigs.

TIP

STRAWBERRY SYRUP IS AVAILABLE FROM MOST DELICATESSENS. IF, HOWEVER, IT'S DIFFICULT TO FIND, USE CLEAR RUNNY HONEY AS A SUBSTITUTE.

SERVE THIS COOLING SALAD AS A SIDE DISH WITH SPICY INDIAN FOOD.

1 To stone the fresh dates, cut each one in half lengthways and remove the stone. Chop the flesh into small dice.

2 Arrange strawberries, cucumber and diced dates on individual side dishes or one large platter.

NUTTY PEAR & FETA SALAD

Clint Brown

This salad makes a light lunch or starter. A popular salad ingredient, watercress creates a base for the crunchy walnuts and feta cheese.

PREPARATION TIME: 10 MINS
COOKING TIME: 5 MINS
SERVES 4

I N G R E D I E N T S

OIL, FOR DEEP FRYING

50 G/2 OZ WALNUT PIECES

1 BUNCH OF WATERCRESS

2 PEARS, PEELED AND COARSELY
CHOPPED

175 G/6 OZ FETA CHEESE, CUBED

FOR THE DRESSING

2 TBLS LEMON JUICE

2 TBLS WALNUT OIL

GROUND BLACK PEPPER

3 Tip the lemon juice and walnut oil into a screw-top jar and season with black pepper. Shake well and pour over the salad.

TIP

NO EXTRA SALT SHOULD BE NEEDED AS FETA CHEESE HAS A SALTINESS OF ITS OWN WHICH IS IMPARTED TO THIS SALAD. FOR A TASTY ALTERNATIVE TO FETA, TRY A STRONG BLUE CHEESE, SUCH AS STILTON OR ROQUEFORT.

 SAUVIGNON, A REFRESHING, DRY WHITE WINE GOES WELL WITH THIS SALAD. CHILL BEFORE DRINKING.

1 Heat oil, add walnuts and fry until lightly golden. Remove with a draining spoon. Drain and cool.

2 Divide the watercress into sprigs. Put in a salad bowl along with the pears, feta cheese and walnuts.

CURLY CHINESE SALAD

Crispy and crunchy, this Curly Chinese Salad
has a ginger and sesame oil dressing which
gives it an oriental flavour.

PREPARATION TIME: 10 MINS
+ CHILLING
SERVES 4

INGREDIENTS

4 LARGE CARROTS, PEELED
4 CELERY STALKS, TRIMMED
½ CUCUMBER
1 BUNCH SPRING ONIONS, TRIMMED
100 G/4 OZ BEANSPROUTS
4 CHINESE LEAVES
FOR THE DRESSING
1 TBLS GRATED GINGER
1 TBLS BROWN SUGAR
3 TBLS RICE VINEGAR OR WINE VINEGAR
1 TBLS SESAME SEED OIL
2 TBLS TOASTED SESAME SEEDS
CUCUMBER SLICES, TO GARNISH
RADISH FLOWERS, TO GARNISH

2 Meanwhile make the dressing: place all the dressing ingredients in a screwtop jar and shake until well blended.

Peter Reilly

3 Drain the carrots, celery, cucumber and spring onions and dry on kitchen paper. Toss with the beansprouts and dressing.

4 Line 4 bowls with the Chinese leaves and spoon in the tossed salad. Garnish with halved cucumber slices and radish flowers.

1 Cut the carrots, celery and cucumber into 7.5 cm/3 in matchsticks. Slice the spring onions in half and cut into 7.5 cm/3 in lengths. Put them all in a bowl of iced water and place in the freezer for ½ hour until they curl.

WATCHPOINT

DON'T PUT THE SALAD VEGETABLES INTO THE FREEZER FOR MORE THAN HALF AN HOUR OR THEY'LL BECOME FROZEN.

TIP

A QUICK WAY TO ROAST SESAME SEEDS IS TO PLACE THEM IN A NON-STICK FRYING-PAN AND GENTLY HEAT THEM — SHAKE THE PAN TO PREVENT THEM STICKING TO THE BOTTOM. THEY CAN THEN BE STORED IN AN AIR-TIGHT JAR FOR UP TO A MONTH AND USED AS REQUIRED.

PINEAPPLE SALAD BOATS

Clint Brown

This summertime special is quick and easy to prepare and its fruit and vegetable ingredients create an exotic impression.

PREPARATION TIME: 30 MINS
SERVES 4

INGREDIENTS

| 1 LARGE PINEAPPLE |
| 300 G/11 OZ COTTAGE CHEESE |
| 1 LARGE CARROT |
| 2 CELERY STALKS, DICED |
| 2 TBLS RAISINS |
| 2 TBLS PUMPKIN SEEDS |
| 2 TBLS PINE KERNELS |
| SALT AND GROUND BLACK PEPPER |
| MINT SPRIGS, TO GARNISH |
| *FOR THE DRESSING* |
| 4 TBLS SALAD OIL |
| 2 TBLS WHITE WINE VINEGAR |

3 Divide and put the mixture onto the 4 pineapple shells. Using 2 palette knives, shape into wedges.

4 Liquidise and sieve the remaining pineapple flesh. Combine the pineapple juice with the oil and vinegar and whisk well.

1 Cut the pineapple into quarters lengthways and scoop out the flesh. Remove and discard the hard centre core and dice half the flesh. Pat the pineapple shells dry.

2 Drain the cottage cheese. Coarsely grate the carrot and mix with the diced pineapple, cottage cheese, celery, raisins, pumpkin seeds and pine kernels. Season.

5 Divide the dressing equally between 4 chilled plates. Put a pineapple boat on each plate on top of the dressing and garnish individually with sprigs of fresh mint.

TIP

ADD 1 TBLS FINELY CHOPPED MINT TO THE PINEAPPLE DRESSING FOR EXTRA COLOUR AND FLAVOUR.

PARISIAN MUSHROOMS

Clint Brown

This simple yet stylish salad combines a wonderful array of tastes and textures and makes the perfect starter for a special meal.

PREPARATION TIME: 15 MINS
SERVES 4

INGREDIENTS

3 TBLS MAYONNAISE
2 TSP DIJON MUSTARD
2 TBLS DOUBLE CREAM
1 TBLS WALNUT OIL
2 TSP WHITE WINE VINEGAR
SALT AND GROUND BLACK PEPPER
225 G/8 OZ BUTTON MUSHROOMS, SLICED
100 G/4 OZ MIXED SALAD LEAVES (RADICCHIO, LOLLO ROSSO, CURLY ENDIVE, CHICORY AND LETTUCE)
2 BACON RASHERS, GRILLED
FRENCH BREAD, TO SERVE

2 Break the salad leaves into pieces reserving 4 small whole radicchio leaves. Wash all the leaves carefully in cold water and either dry using a salad spinner or pat dry with kitchen paper.

3 Toss the lettuce and mushroom mixture together with the remaining walnut oil dressing.

1 Mix together the mayonnaise, mustard and double cream. Then, in a separate bowl, whisk together the oil, vinegar and seasoning. Add just enough of the oil and vinegar to the mayonnaise mixture to give the consistency of thick double cream. Stir the sliced mushrooms into the dressing.

4 To serve, spoon the tossed mushroom mixture generously into the whole radicchio leaves. Snip the bacon into tiny pieces and scatter over the salads. Serve them with chunks of crusty French bread.

TIP

FOR A TASTY VEGETARIAN VERSION OF THIS DELICIOUS SALAD, OMIT THE CRISPY BACON, ADDING INSTEAD CHOPPED, BROWNED HAZELNUTS. USE HAZELNUT OIL INSTEAD OF WALNUT OIL.

GREEK SALAD

Clint Brown

It's very strange that when eating in Greece a Greek salad always seems to appear, no matter what you ordered. Recreate the memory by following this authentic recipe.

PREPARATION TIME: 15 MINS
SERVES 4-6

INGREDIENTS

1 LETTUCE
2 BEEFSTEAK TOMATOES, CUT INTO WEDGES
½ A CUCUMBER, SLICED
1 RED ONION, THINLY SLICED
400 G/14 OZ TINNED ARTICHOKE HEARTS, DRAINED AND QUARTERED
100 G/4 OZ STONED BLACK OLIVES
100 G/4 OZ FETA CHEESE, DICED
FOR THE DRESSING
8 TBLS OLIVE OIL
2 TBLS LEMON JUICE
SALT AND GROUND BLACK PEPPER
1 CLOVE OF GARLIC, CRUSHED
1 TBLS CHOPPED FRESH OREGANO
FOR THE GARNISH
½ A LEMON, CUT INTO WEDGES
4 SPRIGS OF CHERVIL

2 Add the tomatoes, cucumber, onion, artichoke hearts, olives and feta cheese to the bowl.

3 Shake all the dressing ingredients together in a screw top jar and pour over the salad. Toss lightly and garnish with lemon wedges and chervil sprigs.

 THIS SALAD IS IDEAL TO SERVE WITH GREEK DISHES SUCH AS KEBABS, AND GOES ESPECIALLY WELL WITH LAMB. IT CAN ALSO BE SERVED ON ITS OWN AS A LIGHT MAIN MEAL, WITH CRUSTY BREAD TO MOP UP THE DRESSING.

1 Pull the lettuce apart, wash in iced water and spin or drain well. Pat dry with kitchen paper. Put into a large salad bowl.

TIP

EITHER LEAVE THE CUCUMBER SKIN AS IT IS, OR SCORE IT IN LINES BEFORE SLICING, USING A CANELLE KNIFE FOR A PRETTY STRIPED EFFECT.

WALDORF SALAD WITH TUNA

Clint Brown

The traditional Waldorf salad combines apples, celery and walnuts – add some juicy tuna to make a filling meal.

PREPARATION TIME: 15 MINS
SERVES 6

I N G R E D I E N T S

4 RED EATING APPLES

JUICE OF ½ LIME OR LEMON

6 CELERY STICKS, THINLY SLICED

100 G/4 OZ WALNUTS, CHOPPED

400 G/14 OZ TINNED TUNA IN BRINE

6 TBLS MAYONNAISE

4 TBLS SOURED CREAM

SALT AND GROUND BLACK PEPPER

1 ICEBERG LETTUCE

CELERY TOPS, TO GARNISH

3 Take 6 cup-shaped inner leaves from the lettuce and spoon the mixture into each of them. Garnish with celery tops. Serve immediately or keep in the fridge for up to 2 hours.

TIP

FOR A REAL TOUCH OF LUXURY, SUBSTI-TUTE SOME LARGE, COOKED PRAWNS FOR THE TUNA. PEELED ONES CAN BE STIRRED INTO THE SALAD, AND A FEW UNPEELED ONES USED TO GARNISH.

 BAKE SOME JACKET POTATOES AND SERVE THEM WITH BUTTER OR SOURED CREAM, SEA-SONED WITH SALT AND GROUND BLACK PEPPER TO GO WITH THE SALADS. THIS MAKES A TASTY, LATE SUPPER.

1 Cut the apples into quarters, remove the cores then cut into 1 cm/⅓ in pieces. Put in a bowl and toss with the lime or lemon juice to prevent them discolouring. Mix the celery and walnuts in with the apple.

2 Drain the tuna and break into pieces. Stir into the salad. Blend the mayonnaise, soured cream and seasoning in a bowl, and add to the salad.

AVOCADO & PINK GRAPEFRUIT SALAD

Avocados have a wonderful affinity with
grapefruit – the bitter-sweet taste of the pink
grapefruit complements the slightly oily
texture of the avocado.

PREPARATION TIME: 10 MINS
SERVES 4

INGREDIENTS

LAMB'S LETTUCE

2 TBLS VINAIGRETTE DRESSING

2 PINK GRAPEFRUIT

2 AVOCADOS

JUICE OF ½ A LEMON

1 TSP PINK PEPPERCORNS

1 TBLS CHOPPED FRESH MINT

FEW SPRIGS OF MINT, TO GARNISH

1 Toss the lamb's lettuce in 1-2 tsp of the vinaigrette and arrange on 4 serving plates.

2 Using a sharp serrated stainless steel knife, remove the peel and pith from the grapefruit. Slice finely into rings and remove any pips.

3 Slice the avocados into rings and remove the skin. Coat with lemon juice to stop them going brown. Arrange on the plates with the grapefruit, on top of the lettuce.

Peter Reilly

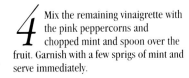

4 Mix the remaining vinaigrette with the pink peppercorns and chopped mint and spoon over the fruit. Garnish with a few sprigs of mint and serve immediately.

TIP

INSTEAD OF LAMB'S LETTUCE USE A BED OF WATERCRESS OR OAK LEAF LETTUCE TO LAY THE FRUIT ON. ALSO, IF YOU CAN FIND THEM, USE COCKTAIL AVOCADOS. THESE LOOK LIKE FAT COURGETTES AND HAVE NO STONE — PERFECT FOR SLICING INTO RINGS. COCKTAIL AVOCADOS ARE ACTUALLY A FREAK OF NATURE — THEY ONLY OCCUR SOMETIMES AND ARE NOT A DIFFERENT VARIETY AT ALL. THEY ARE MARKETED WHEN AVAILABLE, HENCE THEIR COMPARATIVE RARITY.

WATCHPOINT

MAKE SURE THE AVOCADOS ARE RIPE. SLICED INTO RINGS LIKE THIS, UNRIPE FRUIT WOULD STICK TO THE STONES AND THE SLICES WOULD BREAK UP AND LOOK MESSY.

FRILLY BITTER SALAD

Clint Brown

The curl of an endive, the wonder of a Webb's plus a few leafy extras make this excellent leaf salad a treat to eat.

PREPARATION TIME: 10 MINS

SERVES 6

I N G R E D I E N T S

1 OAK-LEAF LETTUCE
1 HEAD RADICCHIO
½ HEAD CURLY ENDIVE
½ HEAD WEBB'S LETTUCE
2 HEADS CHICORY
VINAIGRETTE DRESSING TO SERVE (SEE RECIPE PAGE 8)

1 Hold the oak-leaf lettuce by the stalk and submerge it in a bowl of cold water. Shake off excess water and remove the leaves. Break them into small pieces and set aside.

2 Break the radicchio, endive and Webb's lettuce into pieces before washing. Remove discoloured leaves from the chicory heads and pull apart into separate leaves. Don't bother to wash every leaf.

3 Use a salad spinner to dry all the leaves. Or lay on a clean tea-towel and pat dry. When the leaves are dry, seal in a plastic bag and leave in the fridge until needed.

4 To serve: mix the leaves together in a large bowl. Shake the vinaigrette dressing and then pour over the salad. Toss gently with your hands as salad servers tend to bruise tender leaves. When the leaves are thoroughly coated with the vinaigrette, drain away any excess dressing and transfer dressed leaves to a serving bowl.

 SERVE THIS SALAD AS AN ACCOMPANIMENT TO FISH OR MEAT DISHES.

SMOKED CHICKEN & PASTA

Clint Brown

Don't be chicken about using different pasta
shapes apart from spaghetti – there's no excuse
with all the varieties now available.

PREPARATION TIME: 5 MINS
COOKING TIME: 12 MINS
SERVES 4-6

INGREDIENTS

225 G/8 OZ TRICOLOUR PASTA
SHAPES

SALT AND GROUND BLACK PEPPER

1 TBLS OLIVE OIL

1 ONION, CUT INTO THIN WEDGES

100 G/4 OZ MANGETOUT, CUT INTO
2.5 CM/1 IN DIAMONDS

1 RED PEPPER, SEEDED AND CUT
INTO THIN STRIPS

2 x 150 G/5 OZ SMOKED CHICKEN
BREASTS, SLICED INTO STRIPS

FRENCH BREAD, TO SERVE

FOR THE DRESSING

70 G/2¾ OZ BOURSIN CHEESE

5 TBLS SINGLE CREAM

1 TBLS LEMON JUICE

1 TBLS FRESH CHOPPED PARSLEY

2 Plunge the onion, mangetout and pepper into boiling salted water. Bring the water back to the boil and simmer for 1 minute. Drain the vegetables and cool under cold running water. Drain well and mix vegetables together with the pasta. Transfer to a serving dish and add the chicken.

3 For the dressing: blend all the ingredients together until well mixed. Spoon the dressing over the salad and serve with warm crusty bread.

1 Cook the pasta in boiling salted water for 10-12 minutes, until the pasta is soft, but firm and tender to the bite. Cool under cold running water and drain well. Transfer to a bowl and toss the pasta in the olive oil to stop it sticking together.

 SERVE A LIGHT DRY ITALIAN WINE WITH THIS DISH. VERNACCIO IS A GOOD CHOICE.

SALMON SALAD NICOISE

Ian O'Leary

Adding salmon to this traditional summer salad from the South of France makes it even more appetising. Serve it with a chilled bottle of Provençal white wine.

PREPARATION TIME: 30 MINS
COOKING TIME: 15 MINS
SERVES 4

I N G R E D I E N T S

225 G/8 OZ NEW POTATOES
SALT
225 G/8 OZ FRENCH BEANS, TRIMMED
2 EGGS, HARD BOILED
200 G/7 OZ TINNED SALMON, DRAINED
225 G/8 OZ CHERRY TOMATOES, QUARTERED
1 ROUND LETTUCE
50 G/2 OZ BLACK OLIVES
8 ANCHOVY FILLETS, HALVED
2 TBLS CAPERS, DRAINED
FOR THE DRESSING
7 TBLS OLIVE OIL
2 TBLS TARRAGON VINEGAR
1 TSP DIJON MUSTARD
1 CLOVE OF GARLIC, PEELED AND HALVED
SALT AND GROUND BLACK PEPPER
1 TBLS FRESH CHOPPED PARSLEY

refresh in cold water. Cut the cold potatoes into large chunks. Quarter the eggs and place in a bowl with the green beans, salmon and tomatoes.

2 Place the dressing ingredients in a screw-top jar and shake vigorously to blend. Pour 2 tbls over the mixed ingredients and stir gently.

3 Line a serving plate with lettuce leaves. Spoon on the dressed salad ingredients. Top with olives, anchovies and capers. Pour the remaining dressing over the top, discarding the garlic clove.

TIP

IF THE DRESSING IS MADE WELL IN ADVANCE THE FLAVOURS OF THE HERBS AND GARLIC WILL HAVE A CHANCE TO INFUSE INTO THE OIL AND VINEGAR.

 THIS SALAD CAN EITHER BE SERVED AS AN ACCOMPANYING DISH OR EATEN ON ITS OWN WITH FRENCH BREAD.

1 Place the potatoes in a pan of cold, salted water. Bring to the boil and cook for 15 minutes until tender. Drain and cool in cold water. Cook the beans in boiling water for 7-10 minutes until tender. Drain and

POTATO SALAD

Clint Brown

This is a lively variation of the popular potato salad with the vinaigrette dressing adding a spicy tang to the creamy combination of potato and mayonnaise.

PREPARATION TIME: 10 MINS
COOKING TIME: 10 MINS
SERVES 4

INGREDIENTS

4 MEDIUM-SIZED POTATOES,
SCRUBBED AND DICED

SALT AND GROUND BLACK PEPPER

125 ML/4 FL OZ MAYONNAISE

4 TBLS LEMON JUICE

2 BUNCHES OF SPRING ONIONS,
TRIMMED AND FINELY SLICED

2 HARD-BOILED EGGS, SHELLED AND
CHOPPED

1 LETTUCE

FOR THE VINAIGRETTE

3 TBLS OIL

3 TBLS WHITE WINE VINEGAR

1 TSP DIJON MUSTARD

1 TBLS LEMON JUICE

1 TBLS OREGANO

SALT AND GROUND BLACK PEPPER

1 Boil the diced potatoes in a saucepan of salted water for about 10 minutes until just tender.

2 Combine the vinaigrette ingredients and pour into a screwtop jar. Shake well. Insert a knife into the potato pieces to check if cooked. Drain the potatoes then toss them in the vinaigrette in a bowl and cool.

3 Combine the mayonnaise and lemon juice and season well. When cool, add the potatoes, spring onions and eggs and mix well until all ingredients are well coated with the mayonnaise mixture.

4 Break the lettuce up into large leaves and use to line a salad bowl. Spoon the potato mixture on top of the leaves.

SERVE WITH ANOTHER SALAD OR WITH A SELECTION OF COLD MEATS AND FISH.

MANGETOUT WITH BASIL VINAIGRETTE

Clint Brown

This light crunchy dish with an aromatic dressing will complement meat or fish.

PREPARATION TIME: 5 MINS
COOKING TIME: 5 MINS
SERVES 4

INGREDIENTS

450 G/1 LB MANGETOUT, TOPPED
AND TAILED

FOR THE VINAIGRETTE

1 SMALL ONION, FINELY CHOPPED

2 TBLS FRESH LIME JUICE

2 TBLS RED WINE VINEGAR

1 TSP CLEAR HONEY

2 TBLS VEGETABLE OIL

1 CLOVE OF GARLIC, CRUSHED

1 TBLS FRESH CHOPPED BASIL

SALT AND GROUND BLACK PEPPER

50 G/2 OZ WHOLE, SHELLED AND
SKINNED ALMONDS, TOASTED AND
CHOPPED

2 Whisk in the oil, garlic, chopped basil and seasoning and stir in the chopped almonds.

3 Bring a large saucepan of salted water to the boil, add the mangetout and cook for 1 minute.

1 Combine the chopped onion, lime juice, wine vinegar and clear honey in a saucepan. Cover pan and simmer gently for 2-3 minutes. Leave to cool slightly.

4 Drain the mangetout and transfer to a bowl. Toss in the vinaigrette dressing and serve immediately.

TIP

MANGETOUT ARE BEST EATEN WHEN SLIGHTLY CRUNCHY. DON'T OVERCOOK THEM OTHERWISE ALL THE FLAVOUR AND GOODNESS WILL BE LOST.

ROAST BEEF & PEPPER SALAD

Clint Brown

The subtlety and sweetness of the roasted peppers add an Eastern feel to this colourful main meal salad.

PREPARATION TIME: 15 MINS
COOKING TIME: 10 MINS
SERVES 4

I N G R E D I E N T S

FOR THE SALAD

1 GREEN PEPPER

1 RED PEPPER

1 YELLOW PEPPER

225 G/8 OZ RARE ROAST BEEF, CUT
INTO 1 CM/⅓ IN STRIPS

1 HEAD OF CHICORY, SLICED

3 SPRING ONIONS, SHREDDED

SPRING ONION TASSELS CURLED IN
ICED WATER

FOR THE DRESSING

2 TBLS WHITE WINE VINEGAR

3 TBLS OLIVE OIL

1 TBLS HORSERADISH SAUCE

SALT AND GROUND BLACK PEPPER

3 For the dressing, pour the vinegar and olive oil into a screw-top jar, add the horseradish sauce. Season and shake well, then pour the dressing over the salad.

4 Toss the salad to combine the ingredients and so that the beef and vegetables are evenly covered. Garnish with the spring onion tassels.

SERVE THIS SALAD WITH A
SELECTION OF CRISP LETTUCE
LEAVES OR ON A BED OF
CHINESE NOODLES.

1 Seed and quarter the green, red and yellow peppers. Set them skin side uppermost under a hot grill and cook for 5-10 minutes or until the skin has charred. Plunge the peppers into a bowl of cold water and remove the burnt skin, using a knife.

2 Cut the peppers into thin strips about 6 mm/¼ in wide. Add them to a salad bowl with the strips of beef, sliced chicory and shredded spring onions and toss.

HOT ROOT SALAD

Clint Brown

<u>A hot salad may seem a bit of a contradiction, but tossed in a tasty tarragon dressing it's one that's worth trying.</u>

PREPARATION TIME: 20 MINS
COOKING TIME: 5 MINS
SERVES 4

I N G R E D I E N T S

450 G/1 LB POTATOES, DICED
450 G/1 LB CELERIAC, DICED
100 G/4 OZ RADISHES, CHOPPED
10 CM/4 IN PIECE OF CUCUMBER, DICED
175 G/6 OZ MARINATED HERRING FILLETS, CUT INTO STRIPS
SPRIG OF TARRAGON, TO GARNISH
FOR THE DRESSING
3 TBLS MAYONNAISE
3 TSP TARRAGON VINEGAR
2 TSP TARRAGON MUSTARD
2 TBLS OLIVE OIL
GROUND BLACK PEPPER

2 Transfer the potato and celeriac, along with the chopped radishes, cucumber and strips of marinated herring to a salad bowl.

3 Mix together the dressing ingredients and pour over the salad. Toss together so that the ingredients are well coated and serve warm garnished with fresh tarragon.

1 Put the diced potatoes and celeriac in a pan of salted boiling water. Bring the water back to the boil and cook the vegetables for 5 minutes or until just tender. Drain.

TIP

FOR THOSE WHO DON'T FANCY EATING RAW, MARINATED FISH, THIS RECIPE IS JUST AS GOOD WITH HOT SMOKED FISH SUCH AS TROUT. SIMPLY REMOVE THE SKIN AND BONES AND ADD IN CHUNKS. ALTERNATIVELY USE ANCHOVIES.

ORANGE CELERY WITH WALNUTS

Alan Newnham

This crisp, tangy dish of celery and walnuts
makes an ideal starter or clever side dish.
Completed in 30 minutes, it can be made when
you don't have much time to cook but want to
eat something special.

PREPARATION TIME: 10 MINS
COOKING TIME: 20 MINS
SERVES 4

I N G R E D I E N T S

1 ORANGE
1 LARGE HEAD OF CELERY
25 G/1 OZ BUTTER
25 G/1 OZ WALNUTS
1 TBLS PARSLEY, CHOPPED

Peter Reilly

3 Stir the walnuts into the hot celery and sprinkle with the reserved orange zest and chopped parsley. Serve immediately.

TIP

THE CELERY CAN BE COOKED IN ADVANCE AND REHEATED JUST BEFORE SERVING. COOK THE NUTS AT THE LAST POSSIBLE MOMENT SO THAT THEY STAY CRISP.

1 Using a citrus fruit zester remove the orange zest in shreds. Cut the celery into pieces approximately 2.5 cm/1 in wide.

 PLACE THE CELERY IN A CAS-SEROLE DISH WITH THE ORANGE JUICE. COVER AND MICROWAVE ON HIGH (100%) FOR 6 MINUTES. PUT THE BUTTER AND WALNUTS INTO A MICROWAVE-PROOF BOWL AND COOK FOR 3-4 MINUTES ON HIGH. MIX THE INGREDIENTS TOGETHER AND SERVE.

 SERVE WITH PLAIN BOILED POTATOES AND GRILLED LAMB CHOPS FOR A QUICK AND SIMPLE SUPPER DISH.

2 Squeeze 4 tbls juice from the orange. Place the celery in a stainless steel pan and add the orange juice. Cover and cook for 15 minutes or until tender. Place the butter and walnuts in another pan and cook for 5 minutes or until the walnuts are well browned and crisp.

SEAFOOD RICE SCALLOPS

Clint Brown

Enjoy a taste of the Mediterranean and turn
your thoughts to summer with this fish dish.
The zesty salad can be served as a healthy
addition to almost any meal.

PREPARATION TIME: 10 MINS
+ CHILLING
COOKING TIME: 15 MINS
SERVES 4-6

I N G R E D I E N T S

225 G/8 OZ LONG-GRAIN RICE

PINCH OF SALT

2 COS LETTUCE LEAVES, SHREDDED

2 TOMATOES, SKINNED AND DICED

200 G/7 OZ COOKED PRAWNS

200 G/7 OZ TINNED SWEETCORN

FOR THE DRESSING

8 TBLS OLIVE OIL

2 TBLS LEMON JUICE

ZEST OF 1 LEMON

2 TBLS LIME JUICE

ZEST OF 1 LIME

PINCH OF GROUND FENNEL SEEDS

2 CLOVES OF GARLIC, HALVED

SALT AND GROUND WHITE PEPPER

TO SERVE

4-8 COOKED KING PRAWNS

3 Clean and scald 4 scallop shells and fill with the salad mixture, distributing evenly between shells. Chill in the fridge for 1 hour.

1 Put dressing ingredients into a jar. Shake well. Leave to infuse for 1 hour then remove the garlic.

4 Arrange the king prawns around the scallop shells on a large platter. Serve with dressing.

THIS SALAD CAN ALSO BE SERVED, GARNISHED WITH LETTUCE, LEMON AND FENNEL, WITH FISH KEBABS.

2 Cook the rice in salted water for 12-15 minutes. Drain well. Toss the rice in half the dressing. Cool and stir in remaining salad ingredients.

CHICKEN LIVER TIEDE

Chris King

Hot chicken livers with a cool, crisp salad –
Chicken Liver Tiede makes an attractive
starter. Prepare the salad in advance, and fry
the livers and garlic just before serving.

PREPARATION TIME: 10 MINS +
CHILLING
COOKING TIME: 4 MINS
SERVES 4

I N G R E D I E N T S

2 HEADS OF CHICORY
SMALL BUNCH WATERCRESS
50 G/2 OZ LAMB'S LETTUCE
25 G/1 OZ BUTTER
3 CLOVES OF GARLIC, THINLY SLICED
225 G/8 OZ CHICKEN LIVERS
ROSEMARY SPRIGS
SALT AND GROUND BLACK PEPPER
20 EDIBLE FLOWERS, NASTURTIUMS, BORAGE ETC, TO GARNISH
FOR THE DRESSING
5 TBLS OLIVE OIL
2 TBLS RED WINE VINEGAR
1 TSP WHOLEGRAIN MUSTARD
1 SMALL CLOVE OF GARLIC, FINELY SLIVERED
SALT AND GROUND BLACK PEPPER

2 Heat the butter until it is foaming, add the garlic, chicken livers, a rosemary sprig and seasoning. Fry for 2 minutes on each side, or until livers are browned. Make the dressing: place the olive oil, vinegar, mustard, garlic and seasoning in a jar and shake.

3 Place the chicken livers in-between each bunch of lettuce leaves on the plates. Top each liver with garlic and rosemary. Garnish with flowers and serve with the dressing.

WATCHPOINT

EDIBLE FLOWERS CAN BE GATHERED FROM THE GARDEN, BUT REMEMBER TO MAKE SURE THEY ARE COMPLETELY CLEANED OF INSECTICIDE.

1 Divide the chicory into separate leaves. Finely slice the inside leaves and mix with the watercress. Arrange 5 whole chicory leaves in a wheel spoke fashion on each of 4 plates. Place a small bunch of lamb's lettuce by each chicory leaf. Place a small pile of watercress and chicory leaves in the centre. Cover plates and chill.

PARTY PLATTER

Hilary Moore

An unusual combination of fish, fruit, vegetables
and eggs, this dish is ideal for a buffet party
or light supper.

PREPARATION TIME: 15 MINS
COOKING TIME: 20 MINS
SERVES 4

I N G R E D I E N T S

225 G/8 OZ STREAKY BACON

1 AVOCADO, PEELED AND SLICED

4 TBLS LEMON JUICE

SALT AND GROUND BLACK PEPPER

1 TBLS FINELY CHOPPED FRESH
DILL, PLUS EXTRA TO GARNISH

225 G/8 OZ SMOKED SALMON SLICES,
ROLLED

225 G/8 OZ CHERRY TOMATOES

400 G/14 OZ TINNED ARTICHOKE
HEARTS, DRAINED AND HALVED

1 SMALL RIPE PAWPAW, PEELED,
SEEDED AND SLICED

6 LARGE EGGS

150 ML/¼ PT DOUBLE CREAM

25 G/1 OZ BUTTER

TO SERVE

FRESH BREAD ROLLS

3 Arrange the avocado, smoked salmon, tomatoes, artichoke and pawpaw on a plate, leaving a space for the bacon and the centre for a bowl. Sprinkle the remaining lemon juice over the pawpaw evenly.

1 Grill the bacon for 5 minutes on each side, or until it is very crispy. Drain on kitchen paper, transfer to a plate and keep warm.

2 Place the sliced avocado in a bowl, toss in 1 tbls of the lemon juice, season with salt and pepper and add the finely chopped dill.

4 Beat the eggs in a bowl with the cream and season with the salt and pepper. Heat the butter in a large non-stick frying-pan. Add the eggs and cook over a low heat, stirring constantly, until cooked, which should take approximately 7 minutes.

5 Transfer eggs to a small bowl, garnish with the chopped dill and place in the centre of the plate. Add the bacon to the plate and serve at once with some fresh bread rolls.

SWEETBREAD SALAD

Michael Michaels

Sweetbreads and chicken livers combine to make this tasty salad starter.

PREPARATION TIME: 25 MINS
+ SOAKING
COOKING TIME: 15 MINS
SERVES 6

INGREDIENTS

225 G/8 OZ CALVES' SWEETBREADS

225 G/8 OZ CHICKEN LIVERS

25 G/1 OZ FLOUR, SEASONED

1 EGG, BEATEN

50 G/2 OZ FRESH WHITE
BREADCRUMBS

OIL, FOR DEEP FRYING

MIXTURE OF SALAD LEAVES,
INCLUDING LOLLO ROSSO,
RADICCHIO, CURLY ENDIVE

BUTTER, FOR FRYING

1 TBLS LEMON JUICE

3 TBLS CHOPPED CHIVES, PLUS
WHOLE CHIVES TO GARNISH

FRENCH BREAD, TO SERVE

FOR THE DRESSING

2 TBLS OLIVE OIL

2 TSP LEMON JUICE

SALT AND GROUND BLACK PEPPER

1 Pick over the sweetbreads, remove membranes. Soak in cold water, changing the water regularly until it remains clear. Bring slowly to the boil in a pan of fresh cold water, then drain the sweetbreads well.

2 Put sweetbreads onto a clean tea-towel on a board. Weight down with another board (or plate

with a tin on top). Leave overnight in the fridge. Cut any thick pieces of sweetbread neatly in half, horizontally, to produce flat slices.

3 Cut the livers into pieces, toss in flour and then egg and breadcrumb them. Heat the oil and deep fry the livers a few at a time. Drain on kitchen paper. Toss the salad leaves in a dressing made from oil, lemon and seasoning. Divide among 6 plates.

4 Just before serving, fry the sweetbreads in butter to brown them lightly. They should be firm. Add the lemon juice and a sprinkling of chopped chives to the pan, then divide them and the liver between the plates. Garnish with whole chives. Serve the salads at once, accompanied by slices of crusty French bread.

SWEETBREAD & BACON SALAD

Michael Michaels

A salad of substance. Sweetbread and bacon have their own distinctive flavours which mingle deliciously with the salad leaves.

PREPARATION TIME: 15 MINS
+ SOAKING
COOKING TIME: 25 MINS
SERVES 4

INGREDIENTS

450 G/1 LB CALVES' SWEETBREADS
PINCH OF SALT
25 G/1 OZ BUTTER
225 G/8 OZ STREAKY BACON
BUNCH OF SPRING ONIONS, THICKLY SLICED
ZEST AND JUICE OF 1 LEMON
2 TBLS HAZELNUT OIL
SALT AND GROUND BLACK PEPPER
450 G/1 LB MIXED SALAD LEAVES

2 Cut the rind from the bacon. Grill until very crisp then break up into small pieces.

3 Add the spring onions, lemon zest and juice, plus the hazelnut oil and seasoning to the frying-pan. Cook for a further 2-3 minutes.

1 Soak the sweetbreads in cold water overnight. Drain them thoroughly and put them in a saucepan of salted cold water. Bring to the boil, drain in a colander and refresh with cold water. Remove any membranes and break the sweetbreads into pieces. Fry in the butter over a low heat for 10-15 minutes until tender.

TIP

USE A GOOD MIXTURE OF COLOURFUL AND DIFFERENT SHAPED SALAD LEAVES SUCH AS LOLLO ROSSO, CHICORY AND CURLY ENDIVE. LOOK FOR LETTUCES WITH A FRESH UNWILTED HEAD AND NO DIS-COLORATION IN THE LEAVES.

4 Arrange the salad lettuce leaves in a salad bowl. Tip the contents of the frying-pan over the leaves, toss together and sprinkle with the bacon pieces. Serve immediately.

GAZPACHO MOUSSE

Michael Michaels

The flavours of this light-textured mousse are based on the chilled soup gazpacho, but this is a novel way of serving it.

PREPARATION TIME: 20 MINS
+ SETTING
COOKING TIME: 5 MINS
SERVES 8

I N G R E D I E N T S

700 G/1 LB 8 OZ SMALL, RIPE
TOMATOES

225 G/8 OZ CUCUMBER

2 TBLS EXTRA VIRGIN OLIVE OIL,
PLUS EXTRA FOR GREASING

1 RED PEPPER, SEEDED AND
CHOPPED

2 CLOVES OF GARLIC, CRUSHED

2 TBLS DRY SHERRY

SALT AND GROUND BLACK PEPPER

200 ML/7 FL OZ TOMATO JUICE

1 TBLS POWDERED GELATINE

LEMON SLICES, TO GARNISH

FRESH PARSLEY SPRIGS,
TO GARNISH

3 Pour the tomato juice into a small saucepan and sprinkle over the gelatine. Stand for 5 minutes then place the pan over a low heat for 5-10 minutes or until dissolved.

4 With the motor running, pour the gelatine mixture into the blender in a continuous stream. Make sure it is incorporated evenly into the puréed vegetables. Transfer to a bowl and stand in a cool place.

5 Allow the mixture to begin to set, then spoon into the prepared mould, carefully avoiding dislodging the tomato and cucumber base. Smooth over the top. Refrigerate the mousse for at least 6 hours.

1 Thinly slice two tomatoes and 2.5 cm/1 in of cucumber. Arrange alternately around the base of a lightly oiled 1 L/1¾ pt ring mould overlapping them slightly.

2 Chop the remaining tomatoes and peel and chop the cucumber and place in a food processor or blender with the red pepper, crushed garlic, remaining oil, dry sherry and salt and pepper. Purée to a smooth paste. Leave in the blender.

6 To unmould, dip the base of the mould in hot water for a few seconds then invert on a serving plate. Holding plate and mould shake once to turn out mousse. Garnish with lemon slices and parsley sprigs.

INDEX